Sightings in the Land of the Dead

Barbara Bennett

FUTURECYCLE PRESS

www.futurecycle.org

Cover art, kaleidoscopic treatment of "*Vespula vulgaris*
portrait" (Tim Evison, scientificillsutration.net), plus cover and
interior book design by Diane Kistner (dkistner@futurecycle.org);
author photo by Wendell Thompson; Nikaia text and titling

Published by FutureCycle Press
Hayesville, North Carolina, USA

ISBN 978-1-938853-32-6

Contents

Sightings in the Land of the Dead

They come through the slit where the sun puts the stars to sleep. They bring everything with them—scuffed sorrows, memoried habits, glimpsed bliss—and then release it, bit by bit, after the shock wears off, the delight or anguish. Expectations go first: *every sound a song, every step a dance, every face beloved.* Expectations litter the landscape. No fire. No jewels. More shadow than light.

Graves Lane

A disturbance of air alarms her. She climbs to the second-floor guest room where ashes rest on a bureau, ready for burial. The lavender linen shroud she embroidered with blue forget-me-nots fits snugly over the waxed box the crematory provided. *Little sister*, she whispers, *it's okay to visit, just don't scare me*, and then closes the blinds to the moonlight. When she opens her car door in the morning, sunlight splashes the shape of a five-year-old girl on the passenger seat. Honey, she thinks, her sister's pretend playmate. The air ripples with giggles.

Anderson Funeral Home

That hideous white lining clashes with Mother's casket. I specified cream. The woman ignores her daughter's carping and focuses instead on her grandsons, their new suits, their cowlicks, their plans to fish her lake at sunset. She sees their mother snap at an attendant, their father appease her, the boys make their escape. She senses time shift, her choices—those behind, those ahead—and swims with the bass at dusk.

Waiting Room

If only she'd asked for her purse in her casket or at least for her compact, so she could be sure her hair has returned to its original red and her pin-up girl legs have reshaped. Thank goodness she memorized who she wants to see when. First her son; a parent should never have to bury a child, especially one she can brag on to friends. Next Daddy who always asked for her first when he came home from work, and even after she married he would slip her a twenty when she visited. Then Mother, because Daddy would be hurt if she didn't. Her husband of course. And last her husband's great aunt who willed them the family silver when she passed—sixteen place settings and all the serving pieces. Goodness, his sister put up a fuss, even though it was monogrammed with her maiden initial.

Puget Sound

She wraps a quilt around her shoulders and stands near the window. Her old rooms smell of saltwater and coffee beans. She watches her daughter choosing her clothes before the girl disappears into a clutch of her friends. She wears a linen shift, a necklace of sea glass, a tortoise comb in her hair. At her feet lie sunflowers, cedar, white peaches she gathered for the woman with indigo eyes who may return any day, who smiled and said, *Yes, you will see. Everything. The exact shades of sunsets. Your daughter's first steps. Yours, if you wish.* While she waits, she redreams the colors, their shapes, her being.

Shangri-La

The man stares across the abyss, yearning for a glimpse of his wife. How long since he smelled her lilac scent, the black tea she brewed when he woke, the peppermint lotion she rubbed on his feet after she put the babies to sleep, and never a whiff of rue when he shorted her household account.

She knows this, knows she can call him across, knows his bustle and rumble, his insistences on this and that. So lovely here. The quiet like music. The light a sheen in the west. Willows everywhere. She will call...not yet.

North of Nashville

He jaws with truckers stalled in traffic and guides commuters past back-ups. He enjoys these diversions, but sooner or later he will head for his home ground where he lies under stars from one summer to another. Winters, he beds with bucks. Mornings, he shows the does which oaks drop the most acorns. Nights, possums cross in his light.

Vashon Island

No tree, no vine, no Juliet balcony shades her mother's old bedroom. The girl knows this. If a cat or a bird sat on the sill, she could ignore the shadow. *A cat doesn't harrumph when I pair red shoes with blue leggings,* she protests to her aunt. *A bird doesn't chirp. A daughter of mine should choose yellow. A cloud,* her aunt says dismissively and firmly closes the curtain.

Inside Out

The walls shift from silvery soft to rosy blue. They can chuckle and trill and moo. *I can't name that color to save my life*, the new resident thinks. His roommates grin. Even he sees the humor. At his last address he colored the walls with gunpowder, cocaine and the inside of his head. *Rest*, the roommates insist. The room plays an ètude. *What's next*, he asks when his anxiety lifts. *Birdsong tomorrow*, they reply, *water tonight*.

White Cliffs

Ignoring warnings not to look back, she strides to the edge where she sees mistakes she made mushroom and multiply. Others join her. Not the old and regretful. No, children not ready to leave. Facing what comes from too little perspective, she recruits snow geese and hummingbirds to take the children on trips.

Johnson County Cemetery

The judge returns to watch the women tend the family plot. Some years, features reappear that enchant him. Now, a girl with his first wife's green eyes tugs bindweed from the cedar he planted to shade her grave. He imagines the girl's ponytail loosening, russet hair falling on freckled shoulders. *Something about this place,* he hears her say, sees her glance at her grandmother who hesitates before she admits, *I felt it, too, the first time I came.*

Dark Star

The absence of sky, the glare of galaxies she finds unsettling. She envisioned this scene differently, her first sight of him upon arrival. It wasn't his way to wait, but he knew when to appear. *Set him free. Let him be a star warrior,* a friend had advised to ease her ache at his loss. She balked at letting go of his glow, but she dimmed him down in her thoughts, stopped holding him back. She had feared growing old to his ever-young, but never this undertow of longing and dread.

Los Alamos

He begged for a hole so deep no sound can reach him. What use is death without silence, he pled, eager to quiet the crackle of fire and flesh. He woke to a view of mountains and pear trees. Later, he agreed to haunt a museum. He inhabits shoes, the soles' stillness, the tongues' witness.

Cane Ridge

The professor never expected whiskey barrels and preachers and women's fingers in his britches. His daddy stands under a tree, talking trash with the pickers, a tumbler three fingers full in his hand. His mama's nowhere to be seen, a sure sign of heaven. But why is he back in the woods after fighting his whole life to put it behind? A voice sweet as autumn persimmons reminds him. God knows, he scrapped his way up the ivory tower. Then he used his platform to spit.

Eden

She misses dressing up, misses the slide of silk on skin, the glint of stones at her throat, the prance of pumps underfoot. The wild patch she tends bores her. Pa would have coaxed ramp and polk as if it were spring onions and spinach. Mam would have gathered the weeds for a bitter green stew. She loathes kitchen and yard work, but loathing is discouraged here where she's stuck. When visitors glance her way in the garden, she picks violets or digs sassafras roots.

Foul Bay

Except for the wind that blows east, ever east, as if wind owns only
one direction, he enjoys the ocean view; but he knows westerlies create
steering flows and cyclones. No coward, he requested burial at sea,
not another route to follow or cross. He joined the navy to escape a
stepfather's fists and learned how to navigate sea lanes and trade
winds. He married and learned how to fail a pretty wife and many
daughters, but not how to grieve a lost son.

Grand Banks

Day in, day out, the same questions halo up the coast. *Not done yet? What's the holdup?* As if he will learn the measurements of warm and wind that shift foggy to vivid. He ducks answering. He knows the alchemy of bottomland fields, of winter seeping from soil. He remembers his mother's climb up briared banks to reach safer ground with him in tow. His wives pushed him along, as well. He feared their fierceness, their skill, his want of both. The mossy light he prefers obscures clarity, passion, rebuke.

Grand Prairie

She rests beside a river that flows through fields her husband har-
vested, where monarchs feed on ironweed. Her cane taps a silent beat
on granite. The rhythm reminds butterflies to rise and ride the wind
south. Children murmur her name. Still she keeps time, steady and
quiet, as one by one their voices fall silent. Somewhere a girl slides feet
into slippers her mother wore to a dance. Somewhere a boy lies to his
mother. Somewhere it is always September.

Isle of Skye

The old man wades the lochs of his ancestors, measuring the temperature of glaciers. No one wants the job from one ice age to the next. Mists rise like ground fog in August. He recalls corn shucked and tossed into wagons, the rough play of men, girls whose aprons covered their softness. The preachers who promised heaven or hell never mentioned a place so cold the only sign of spring is a lighter shade of lichen. Memories of hired hands he bullied, women he scorned, children he struck fail to warm him.

Lexington

Veterans fill every byway, and more arrive each day. The whole Earth, it seems, is an assembly line for soldiers: Afghan, American, Apache, Argentine, Austrian, and those just the A's. The general needs the rest, of course. But then what? He declines to oversee an expansion, accustomed though he is to duty. Naming roses pleases him. *New Dawn, Peace, Agnes* for the daughter who died before he did.

Glen Echo

Tend the wounded. Find the missing. Clean the dead. Work she grasps.
So little to do here: cut flowers and arrange them, stroll by the sea. She
harvests wisteria and lemongrass to weave into baskets and collects
geodes to fill with sweet sage and cream-colored roses. Mornings, she
re-shells beaches or laps the Atlantic.

Golden Valley

When he arrives, timber fills the valley, trees nearly as tall as the cliffs and straighter. He envisions a dock where the river meets the lake, a lodge and cabins. The memory remains of his hands guiding a saw and a plane. The work will last, he imagines, until Mary comes with the children. He clears both sides of the river before pausing. An age has passed. More. Watching light fill the ridges, he grasps at last that his wife and his seed are not his to collect or command.

Icarian Sea

It wasn't easy finding a site that suits him, arriving early and bruised as he did. He tried sailing mountain passes, coaching fledglings, clearing the air after rain. There were complaints: pilots uneasy, weather vanes tipsy, a breath of regret in the wind. Only water soothes him and even that was a case for trial and error: springs too cheerful, rivers too narrow, lakes humdrum. Here, he tracks tides, watches the moon rise and recede, plays chase with shearwater birds among starlit breakers.

Yellow World

She spins spider silk in a grove of silver aspen. Leaves laugh; threads dance in her fingers. The loom whispers *Beauty, beauty, beauty* as it waits for the skeins. Her sisters who know her true name and nature bristle when her lovers arrive bearing pails of goat milk, bales of sea-grass, requests for forgiveness or favors. *Go away,* the women hiss. *A proper warp makes all the difference.*

Black Mountain

The summons comes as a hum. She feels more than hears it. A snatch of a chant plagues her as she joins the gathering. *It's raining. It's raining. My clothes are getting wet. My clothes are getting wet.* She forgets what it means. Voices throng the ruined mountains, the misspent rivers, the smoked forests. The chorus crescendos and holds, not as aria, as moan.

Highway 99 and Route 44

He wants to wake yesterday and say, *Let's skip the road trip. Let's sleep late, instead.* He wants to finish the addition they planned, a woodshop for him, a skylight and studio for her, a bath with two of everything for the two of them. He wants her ex to let him raise her kids. He does not want his father to say he is young and will find someone else. He does not want his broken bones to mend. He does not want to be the one left.

Sad River

The car strikes her bike. Metal and glass and screams rip the sky. *Bethany, Jacob*, she weeps. Morning stars flare. A current sweeps her to shore. Mothers stream from the forest to hold her. They wade through the water and collect tumbled pebbles. On each, they carve a name and pile them all at her feet. *Who are they*, she asks. *Your children's children*, they sing, *their children, their children's children.*

About FutureCycle Press

FutureCycle Press is dedicated to publishing lasting English-language poetry and flash fiction books, chapbooks, and anthologies in both print-on-demand and ebook formats. Founded in 2007 by long-time independent editor/publishers and partners Diane Kistner and Robert S. King, the press incorporated as a nonprofit in 2012. A number of our editors are distinguished poets and writers in their own right, and we have been actively involved in the small press movement going back to the early seventies.

The FutureCycle Poetry Book Prize and honorarium is awarded annually for the best full-length volume of poetry we publish in a calendar year. Introduced in 2013, our Good Works projects are devoted to issues of universal significance, with all proceeds donated to a related worthy cause. Our Selected Poems series highlights contemporary poets with a substantial body of work to their credit. Our flash fiction line presents quick reads that can be serious or light-hearted, irreverent or quirky, fantastic or futuristic, or just plain fun.

We are dedicated to giving all of the authors we publish the care their work deserves, making our catalog of titles the most diverse and distinguished it can be, and paying forward any earnings to fund more great books.

We've learned a few things about independent publishing over the years. We've also evolved a unique, resilient publishing model that allows us to focus mainly on vetting and preserving for posterity the most books of exceptional quality without becoming overwhelmed with bookkeeping and mailing, fundraising activities, or taxing editorial and production "bubbles." To find out more about what we are doing, come see us at www.futurecycle.org.

www.ingramcontent.com/pod-product-compliance
Lightning Source LLC
Chambersburg PA
CBHW061201040426
42445CB00013B/1770